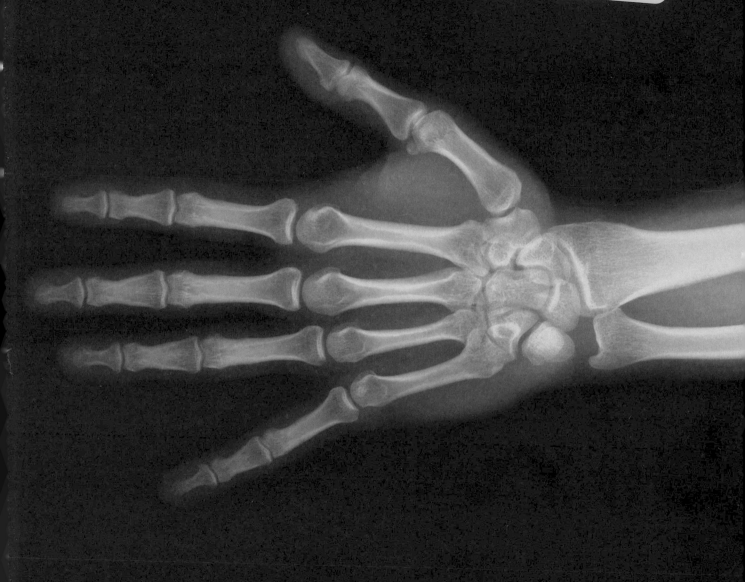

FIND OUT ABOUT
THE BODY

With 17 projects and more than 250 pictures

STEVE PARKER

ARMADILLO

This edition is published by Armadillo,
an imprint of Anness Publishing Ltd, Blaby Road,
Wigston, Leicestershire LE18 4SE;
info@anness.com

www.annesspublishing.com

If you like the images in this book and would like to investigate using them for
publishing, promotions or advertising, please visit our website
www.practicalpictures.com for more information.

© Anness Publishing Ltd 2012

A CIP catalogue record for this book is available from the British Library.

Publisher: Joanna Lorenz
Senior Editor: Caroline Beattie
Photographer: John Freeman
Stylist: Thomasina Smith
Designer: Caroline Reeves
Picture Researcher: Liz Eddison
Illustrator: Alisa Tingley
Production Controller: Ben Worley

PUBLISHER'S NOTE

Although the advice and information in this book are believed to be
accurate and true at the time of going to press, neither the authors nor
the publisher can accept any legal responsibility or liability for any
errors or omissions that may have been made nor for any
inaccuracies nor for any loss, harm or injury that comes about
from following instructions or advice in this book.

Manufacturer: Anness Publishing Ltd, Blaby Road,
Wigston, Leicestershire LE18 4SE, England
For Product Tracking go to:
www.annesspublishing.com/tracking
Batch: 0354-21018-1127

The publishers
would like to thank
Laura Akinpelumi,
Jaki Bell, Katie Blue, Jackie
Ishiekwene, Jemmy Jibowa, Daniel
Johnson, Lauren Kendrick, Jon Leaning,
Jermaine Makinde, Hanife Manur, Yew Hong
Mo, Louise Morgan, Vishal Pithia, Graham Roberts,
Amy Stone, Charlie Thompson, Almarie Tonge, Ini
Usoro, Gary Waters, Joe Westbrook from St John the Baptist
C. of E. Primary School, Maria Bloodworth, Maxine Levy, Erin
Mccarthy and Peter Watson from Walnut Tree Walk Primary School,
and Andrew Brown, Lee and Reece Johnson,
Rebekah Murrell and Magdalena Nawroka-Weekes.

CONTENTS

PICTURE CREDITS

b=bottom, t=top, m=middle, l=left, r=right

Biophoto Associates: pages 19tl, 22mr, 24mb and mr, 30tr, 37tl, 39m, 62r and b, 63tl. P Gordon: page 36br.
Alistair Hughes: page 10tl. Andrew Syred/Microscopix Photolibrary: pages 10br, 11tr, 37tl, 42tl, 51 inset, 56tl, 62l.
Angela Hampton/Reflections Photolibrary: page 63br; Jennie Woodcock/Reflections Photolibrary: pages 11mr, 24tl. Alfred Pasieka/Science Picture Library: pages 19mt, 28br; A. B. Dowsett/Science Picture Library: page 51t; John Reader/Science Picture Library: page 37tr. Tony Stone Images/David Madison: page 58tl; Tony Stone Images/Chris Harvey: page 63bl. Trip/K. Cardwell: page 9bl; Trip/A. M. Bazalik: page 23bl; Trip/R. Williamson: page 44tr. Zefa Pictures: pages 23bm, 28bl, 48tl.

YOUR BODY

The body has a strong framework of bones, to hold it up. There are more than 200 bones inside the body, and hundreds of other bits and pieces, too.

WHAT do you see most each day? Schoolwork, perhaps? Or television? Most people spend a long time each day looking at bodies – human bodies belonging to family, friends, teachers, supermarket staff and many other people you meet every day. You watch these bodies move about, walk and talk, eat, laugh, cry and carry out their daily lives. You probably know a lot about the people you see every day. But how much do you know about their bodies – and about your own body? Why does the human body have two arms and two legs, with the head on top? Why does it have hair and fingernails? How does it run, jump and speak? What happens to food after it is swallowed? And how does the body work inside?

Bodies change through their lives. They grow bigger, then after many years, they may shrink slightly. Can you remember how small you were, and how big and tall everyone else seemed, when you were a baby? What are your earliest memories?

Different types

There are two main kinds of human body, male and female. The female ones are called girls when young and women when grown up. The male ones are called boys when young and men when grown up.

Different shapes

Bodies vary on the outside, even when they are all the same age. Some are taller than others. Some have different shades of hair, eyes and skin. But on the inside, bodies are all much the same.

Sometimes the body needs to eat. Food gives it energy and nutrients, for moving about, growing and carrying out all its living processes.

Sometimes the body stays still. It can be standing up, sitting or lying down when it does this. Yet inside, parts like the heart are still moving.

Sometimes the body does active things, like running. It can jog slowly or sprint fast, and kick or throw a ball at the same time!

This book answers all these questions, and many more. It shows how your eyes work, what your bones look like, how your heart beats, and what happens in your brain. Learning about the body is easy, because you always have one to study!

Sometimes the body rests and sleeps. Every body needs to sleep, usually at night. Younger bodies generally need more sleep than older ones.

FACT BOX
• Each human body is a member of the animal group, or species, that scientists call *Homo sapiens* ("Wise human").

• There are about 7,000 million human bin the world. This compares with over 1,000 million sheep, and up to 500 million dogs.

• No animals have spread to as many places in the world as humans. People live in snowy polar lands, in steamy tropical forests, in deserts and on high mountains. One of the most widespread animals, after us, is the house mouse.

Sometimes the body does quiet things, like reading, listening to music, drawing pictures or solving puzzles. It can learn lots of new skills and information at this time.

MEASURING YOUR BODY

To measure your weight, simply stand on some weighing scales! Take off shoes and thick clothes, like a coat, since these make you seem heavier. Do not worry about taking off light clothes like T-shirts. Note your weight in kilograms or pounds.

Ｈow tall are you? How much do you weigh? What size shoes do you take? You may know the answers to these questions – or you can find out by measuring. But what about your hat, collar or glove size? People measure the body to find out its size and shape, for many reasons. A doctor measures the weight of a new baby to make sure it is healthy and growing well. An optician measures a person's eyes, for spectacles. A tailor measures neck, waist, chest, arms and legs, to make well-fitting clothes. How do you measure up?

M A T E R I A L S

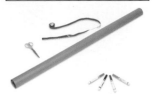

You will need: tape measure, large roll of paper (such as the back of an unwanted roll of untreated wallpaper), felt-tipped pens, scissors.

Draw a graph of your body measurements over months, or even years.

Measure parts of your body

1 Measure around the waist at the level you would wear a belt.

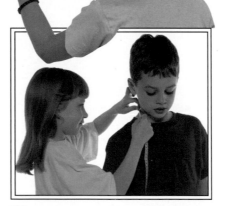

2 Measure around the neck, at its narrowest point.

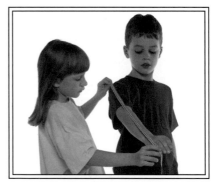

3 Measure the arm from the point of the shoulder to the wrist.

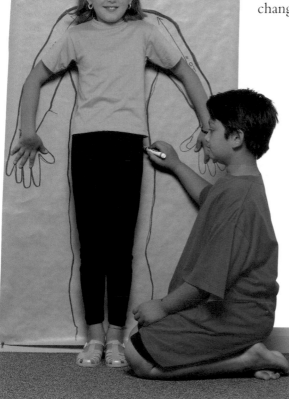

You could make a chart of your body's different measurements over the years. Use different pens on the graph to plot height, weight, waist size and so on. Measure yourself at regular times, such as every three months, or on your birthday, or on the last day of each school term. Which measurement changes most, and which alters least?

Same age, different size
Get together with some friends of the same age (in years). How much variation is there between you all in height, or weight? Try the same test on children who are much younger, such as two years old. Do the same for grown-ups who are 20 years old, for example. Which age shows the most variation?

Body outline
Trace around the whole body with a felt-tipped pen. Trace around friends, too. Label each tracing with the date. Next time, use different shades of pen. Who has grown the most?

Feet and hands
Draw carefully around your foot and hand. Do the same for friends. Who has the thinnest fingers, the widest palm or the thickest wrist?

FACES

Look in the mirror. Which part of your body do you see? Probably, your face. This is the most-looked-at part of anybody's body, for many reasons. Faces are truly fascinating. They show people's moods – happy, sad, pleased, worried, tired or thoughtful. Tiny movements of the eyebrows and eyelids can mean a lot, like surprise or anger. A flicker around the lips may mean that a smile is coming, or a frown. In most countries a nod of the head indicates yes, and a shake means no. When we listen to people speak, we also watch the movements of their mouths and lips. This helps us to make out what they say. Also, the rest of the body is often covered by clothes, so you cannot see it!

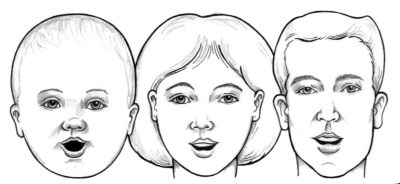

How faces change with age

As you grow, whether male or female, your face gets bigger. It also changes its proportions. A baby's face is small compared to the size of its whole head. Its eyes and forehead are big, its nose and mouth are small. In a grown-up, the nose and mouth take up more of the face, and the face takes up over half of the front of the head.

Two-sided face

Both sides of a face look the same. They could be perfect mirror-images of each other. But are they exactly identical – that is, are they symmetrical? Here is a normal photograph of a boy. Compare it with the following faces.

Two right sides

The left side of this photograph has been cut away, and replaced with a reversed or swapped-over version of the right side. So this face is the boy's right half plus a mirror-image of it. Does it look like the real face to its left?

Two left sides

In this version, the right side of the photograph is replaced by a reversed version of the left side. So this shows the face's left half plus a mirror-image of it. Does it look more like the real face than the two-right-sides one on the left?

Young and old

A baby's face usually has smooth, soft skin. After many years, the skin may develop wrinkles and lines. This is entirely natural. It is more likely to happen if the person spends a lot of time out in the sun and wind.

FACT BOX

• Most grown-ups can recognize at least 500 people from their faces. This includes family and friends, and also famous faces like stars of music, movies and sports.

• When you see your face in a mirror, it is not the face that other people see. It is reversed (swapped), left to right. This is why some people are surprised by the way they look in photographs.

• To see yourself as others see you, study a photograph of yourself. Compare it with your face in a mirror. Which one do you like best? Is it the most familiar one?

Disguise

If you want to disguise yourself, start with your face. This is the part that other people recognize most. You could wear a large hat, and perhaps add or take off your spectacles. A beard or a moustache might help, plus a scarf. The more of your face that you cover up, the less recognizable you become.

SKIN, HAIR AND NAILS

THE body is totally covered in skin – well, not quite. There are openings for parts such as the eyes, ears, nose and mouth. But the rest is skin. This marvellous body covering is flexible and stretchy, so you can move. It keeps body fluids and other needed substances inside. It keeps germs, dirt and unwanted substances outside. Skin is always being worn away as you move about, get washed and dressed, grip and hold things, and rub against them. But skin is always growing just under the surface, to replace the bits that are worn away. Most of the skin over the body is covered in hairs. Some of these hairs are thick and easily seen, like the hairs on your head. Other hairs are so small you need a magnifier to see them. Only a few parts of the body are truly hairless, like the palms of the hands and the soles of the feet.

Hair, like skin, keeps growing. Most people have about 100,000 hairs on their head. Each one grows for a couple of years. It could reach more than 1 metre (1 yard) in length. Then it falls out and is replaced by a new hair.

With a magnifier, look very closely at the skin on different parts of the body. See how it varies. Some parts are smooth and flat. Others have lines and creases, especially around joints, where the skin stretches and bends a lot.

Handy skin
A hand has different kinds of skin – smooth, creased, thick, thin, hairless and hairy, as well as nails. Skin, hair and nails are all made from the substance called keratin. This is the same stuff that makes the claws, hooves and horns of other animals.

Close to skin
Under a powerful microscope, even the smoothest skin has tiny hills and valleys, lines and creases. Sweat oozes up through the tiny dot-like holes, called sweat pores.

Even closer to skin
The individual flakes of skin are microscopic dead cells, flattened and filled with tough keratin. They fall off the body by the thousand every minute.

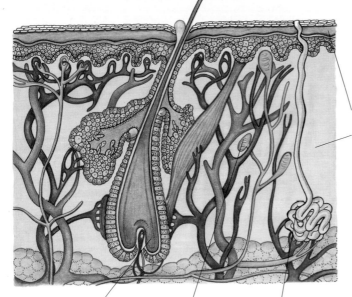

Giant hair

When you get this close to a hair, it does not look so smooth and shiny! The whole hair is dead, except for its very lowest part, the root, under the skin's surface.

Epidermis

Dermis

Hair root   *Touch sensor*   *Sweat gland*

Inside skin

Skin has two layers. The upper one is the epidermis. This keeps growing, to replace flakes of skin that are worn away. The lower layer is the dermis. It has tiny touch sensors, nerves and blood vessels.

Skin tone

Different shades of skin and hair are due to different amounts of very dark pigment, a substance called melanin. Small patches of skin with slightly more melanin than surrounding skin are called freckles.

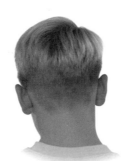

FACT BOX

• Spread out flat, the skin of a grown-up person would cover about 2 square metres (21 square feet), the area of an office desk.

• The thickest skin is on the soles of the feet. In someone who does not wear shoes, it grows even thicker, for extra protection. It may be more than 5 millimetres ($\frac{1}{4}$ inch) thick.

• On the eyelids. the skin is less than half a millimetre (two-hundredths of an inch) thick.

• An average hair grows about 1 millimetre (four-hundredths of an inch) every three days.

• An average fingernail grows 1 millimetre (four-hundredths of an inch) every seven days.

Hair types

Hairs can be dark or light, and thick (coarse) or thin (fine), and straight, wavy or curly. The length of the hair and the style of its cut greatly alter its appearance.

TOUCH AND FEELING

MATERIALS

You will need: two pencils with sharp points, ruler, two elastic rubber bands, non-permanent ink pad, paper, magnifier.

WHEN you touch something, your skin tells you many features about it. You can feel whether it is hard or soft, hot or cold, rough or smooth, wet or dry. Touch comes from millions of microscopic touch sensors all over your skin. These detect light contact and heavy pressure, movement, temperature and other features. They send nerve signals to your brain, telling you what you are feeling. However, the touch sensors are not spread evenly all over the body. Some areas of skin have more of them, so they are more sensitive than other areas. Fingertips, with their swirly ridges, are very sensitive indeed to the slightest touch.

Sensitive points

1 Fix the pencils firmly to the ruler with the elastic bands. Make one pencil point line up exactly with the 0 on the ruler scale.

2 Ask a friend to close their eyes, or use a blindfold. Touch both pencil points gently at the same time on separate patches of skin.

3 Does the friend feel two points, or one? Try again, reducing the gap between the pencils. The most sensitive skin detects the smallest gap.

Stamping fingerprints

1 Swirly skin-ridge patterns on the fingers are called fingerprints. To see them, dab a finger or thumb on the ink pad with a rolling motion.

2 With the same rolling motion, dab the finger or thumb on to a strip of card. This transfers the ink and makes the print.

3 Make prints for all of your fingers and thumbs, and label them. Ask some friends to make their own sets of fingerprints, too.

Studying fingerprints

Look at the sets of prints carefully, using a magnifying glass. See how they have various patterns. These are called whorls (which are like part-spirals), arches and loops. With practice, can you recognize your own prints? Are the prints of your family members quite similar to your own?

Every print is different

No two people in the whole world have the same fingerprints. We all have different print patterns. This is why fingerprints can be used to prove that a person has been at a certain place. When the fingers touch a surface, they leave tiny traces of natural skin oil and sweat, in the same pattern as the prints. A special powder reveals the pattern.

EYES AND SEEING

THE body has five main senses, which tell it about its surroundings. They are touch, seeing, hearing, smell and taste. Seeing with the eyes is the most informative sense. About half of the total knowledge and memories in the brain gets there through the eyes. This happens when you read words, and look at pictures and diagrams, as you are doing now, as well as seeing faces, people, objects and scenes around you. The eyes identify patterns of light rays, turn these into nerve signals, and send them to the brain. Since seeing is so important, everyone should have an eye test every year or two. (People who are blind or cannot see clearly use their other senses more, like hearing and touch.)

The eyes have their own small lenses, which focus light rays to give you a clear view. Extra lenses like those in binoculars make things look larger and nearer.

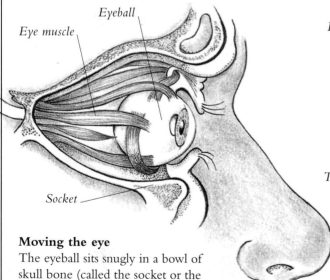

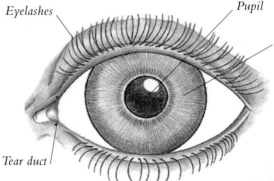

Moving the eye
The eyeball sits snugly in a bowl of skull bone (called the socket or the orbit). Six small muscles join each eye to the bone at the back. They pull the eyeball in different ways to make it twist and swivel. This is how you look up, down and to each side.

Look into my eyes …
Most of the eyeball is behind skin and skull bone, inside the head. The dark spot in the middle is a hole, the pupil, where light goes into the eye. Eyelashes keep dust off the eye's sensitive front surface. Eyelids blink to wipe tear fluid over the eye and to wash away dust, dirt and germs.

14

Inside the eye

The cutaway view below shows the small and delicate parts inside the eyeball. Light comes in through the clear dome-shaped cornea at the front, and passes through the pupil, the circular hole in the iris. The light rays are focused (bent), so they shine a clear, sharp image onto the back of the eye. This is lined by the retina which contains millions of light-sensitive cells. When the cells receive light rays, they create nerve signals which pass along the optic nerve to the brain.

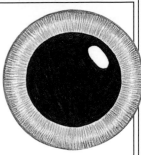

Iris and pupil

The eye's inside is very sensitive. Too much light is harmful. So the pupil gets small in bright light, to prevent damage. It widens in dim conditions, to see better in the dark. This happens by a change in size of the iris, the ring of muscle around the pupil.

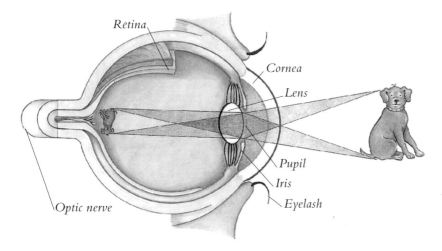

Retina
Cornea
Lens
Pupil
Iris
Eyelash
Optic nerve

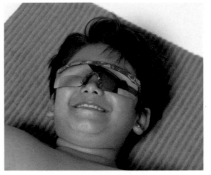

Eye care

Eyes can be harmed by dust, splashes of chemicals, objects like thrown stones or flies, and too much light – including bright sunshine. It is always wise to protect your eyes with goggles or sunglasses.

Brown or blue eyes?

Eyes are a particular shade because of the iris. It may be brown, green, blue, grey or nearly black. All new babies have blue eyes. It takes several months for their final shade to develop.

TRICKING THE EYES

E<small>YES</small> cannot see everything, all around, all the time. When you look straight at something, to see its details, you miss what goes on around the sides. Also, we can make trick patterns and movements that the eye does not see in normal life. These fool the eye – rather, they fool the brain. It is your brain that analyses the nerve signals from the eyes, identifies objects and movements, and understands what you see.

MATERIALS

You will need: card, pair of compasses, pencil, felt-tipped pen, scissors, cocktail stick or toothpick.

This picture shows a white triangle – or does it? There seems to be a solid white triangle blocking out parts of the black discs and black triangle. The brain makes it up, as the most sensible reason for the pattern.

Optical illusions trick the brain. At one end, this looks like three round tubes. But at the other end, it looks like two square tubes. The pattern of lines on paper creates a puzzling picture which could not be a real object.

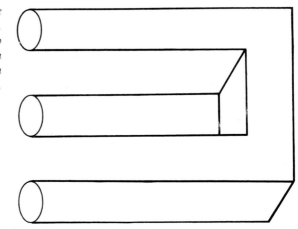

Hole-in-the-head?

If the brain cannot understand all of a scene, it makes up hidden parts and fills the gaps. Do that here, and the boy has an arrow through his head! But common sense tells us it is a trick. Sure enough, the arrow parts are joined by a curved piece of wire, hidden in his hair.

Spiral spinner

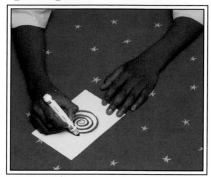

1 For the spiral spinner, draw a circle on the card using the compasses. Draw a spiral shape with the pencil first, to get the right shape, then follow the line with the felt-tipped pen.

2 Carefully cut the card around the circle's edge, to make a disc with the spiral on it. Pierce the middle of the disc with the cocktail stick, making sure the stick is a tight fit.

3 Spin the disc like a toy top. One way, the line seems to move inwards and disappear into the stick. The other way, it seems to move out and fall off the disc's edge. Of course, it really goes nowhere!

Moving circles

1 For moving circles, draw several sets of spirals or circles on two large white cardboard sheets. Make them clear and vivid. Do the same again, to make a second set. Hold one cardboard sheet and move the other in small circles.

2 Can you make sense of what you see? Do the circles seem to rotate? This is a very unusual scene that the brain has trouble understanding. What effect do you see if you move both cards in small circles?

Rainbow wheel

1 For a rainbow wheel, divide a disc of card 10 centimetres (4 inches) across into seven equal slices or segments (about 51° each). Shade in the segments like a rainbow or spectrum in the correct order: red, orange, yellow, green, blue, indigo, violet.

2 Pierce the middle with a cocktail stick or toothpick, and spin fast. The rainbow merges into white (or perhaps grey). This is because white light is a mixture of many different rainbow hues of light – the spectrum. The spinning wheel merges this spectrum to form white.

EARS AND HEARING

Listen carefully. What can you hear? Even in the quietest place, there are sounds – wind, rustling leaves, birds singing, a car or a plane. Hearing is the body sense that detects sound waves. These are invisible "ripples" that pass out from any object making a noise, whether it is a cat purrrrrrring or a hi-fi pounding out music. The ripples are vibrations, or fast to-and-fro movements, of the tiny floating molecules which make up air. Vibrations pass through air into your ears, which are inside the head, almost behind the eyes. The inner parts of the ears detect the vibrations and change them into nerve signals, which go to the brain. Parts of the inner ears, called semicircular canals, also help to sense movements and gravity, to help with the process of keeping your balance.

Protect your ears from extreme cold, or too-loud sounds, or very dusty air, with ear muffs. Like eyes, ears are delicate and easily harmed. Never push or poke anything into the ear canal. It should keep itself clean naturally.

Ear shapes

What we call "the ear" has little to do with hearing. It is simply a curved flap of skin and cartilage (gristle) on the side of the head. Ears come in many shapes and sizes, but this has little effect on hearing. They gather sound waves and funnel them into the ear canal.

Listen up

Whenever you hear sounds, sound waves travel straight down your outer ear canal. This is the dark hole in the outer ear, and it is about 3 centimetres (1¼ inches) long. At its end a thin piece of skin is stretched across, called the eardrum (shown on the opposite page). It is about the size of your fingernail. The sound waves bounce off the eardrum and make it vibrate, or shake to and fro.

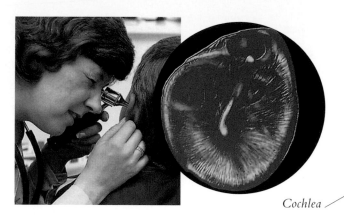

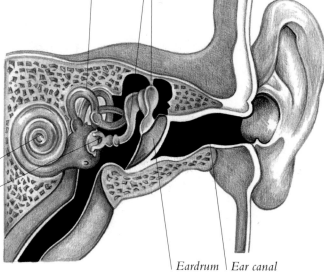

Semicircular canal   Anvil   Hammer

Cochlea

Stirrup

Eardrum   Ear canal

A doctor looks into the ear using an otoscope, to check for infections or other problems. The eardrum looks like a patch of thin reddish skin, with the hammer bone just behind it.

Low and high sounds

Some sounds are deep and booming, like thunder or a big drum. Others are high and shrill, such as a piercing scream or a cymbal. This is called pitch or frequency, and it is measured in Hertz (Hz). Human ears hear many frequencies, from the deepest notes at 25 Hz to extremely high ones at 15,000 Hz. In general, when big objects vibrate, they make deeper sounds. A large handbell has a lower sound or musical note than a small handbell. Some animals can hear ultrasounds. These are sounds too high-pitched for our ears to detect, like the squeaks of bats.

Inside the ear

Sound vibrations hit the eardrum and pass along three tiny bones, the hammer, anvil and stirrup, to fluid inside the snail-shaped cochlea. Here the vibrations are turned into nerve signals that go along the cochlear nerve to the brain.

Not too loud

The loudness of a sound is called its volume. It is measured in decibels. Sounds louder than about 85–90 decibels can damage the delicate inner parts of the ear, especially if they go on for a long time. So too-loud earphones or music speakers can harm your hearing. People who work near noisy machines, such as road drills and aircraft, wear earplugs and ear-defenders to cut out the sound and protect their hearing.

LOUD AND QUIET

WHEN you hear a very loud noise, like a banging drum, do you turn away and put your hands over your ears? And when you try to hear something very quiet, like a whisper, do you lean forward and turn one ear towards it? Your body's position and movements help you to hear, and to stop your ears being damaged by loud noises. These projects show how you can make sounds seem louder, and how you can see the vibrations of sound waves. The megaphone shown below is a funnel shape, like an extra-big mouth. It collects sound waves from your voice and makes them spread forwards in one direction only. It also works the other way round, as an extra-big ear called an ear trumpet, which collects lots of sound waves.

Drums are fun, but loud. The harder you hit them, the more the drum head (skin) vibrates, and the noisier it becomes. Bigger drums make lower, deeper bangs.

Whispers are quiet, and usually secret. If there are other sounds, like people talking or music playing, you may have to get very close to the whisperer.

Megaphone

1 Carefully cut out this shape from a large sheet of thin cardboard. When rolled up and taped, it will form a funnel shape which can be used as a megaphone or ear trumpet.

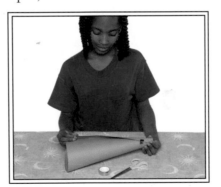

2 Roll the cardboard into a funnel or cone shape. Make the big end as wide as possible, and the small end about 3-4 centimetres (1½ inches) wide. Tape the cardboard in position.

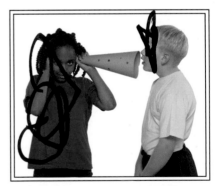

3 Listen normally to your friend talking, then listen using the funnel as an ear trumpet. Talk to your friend normally, then through the megaphone. Does it help you hear?

Copy your ear

1 Cover one side of the pan with a sheet of clear film or plastic wrap. Make sure it is stretched tightly across, with no creases. If necessary, fix it to the pan with adhesive tape.

2 Push the short end of one straw into the long end of another. Carefully cut a few slits in the remaining long end so it splays out, ready for the table-tennis ball.

3 Tape the table-tennis ball on to the folded-back slits in the straw. Bend the straws at right angles and secure with tape. Tape the other straw to the clear film or wrap as shown.

The sheet of clear film or plastic wrap works like your eardrum. It vibrates when sound waves hit it.

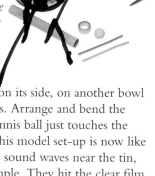

MATERIALS

You will need: circular pan with loose base removed (such as for baking a cake), clear film or plastic wrap, adhesive tape, bendy plastic drinking straws, scissors, table-tennis ball, bowl of water.

The straw works like your tiny ear bones. It passes vibrations along to the next part.

The bowl of water is like your cochlea. The vibrations spread as ripples across it.

4 Support the pan on its side, on another bowl or on some books. Arrange and bend the straws so the table-tennis ball just touches the water in the bowl. This model set-up is now like your ear! Make some sound waves near the tin, by clapping, for example. They hit the clear film, which works like your eardrum. This vibrates and sends the vibrations along the straws, which work like the tiny ear bones. The ball makes ripples in the bowl, which is like the fluid-filled cochlea. As a result, you can actually see sound waves.

NOSE AND SMELL

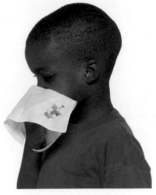

CAN you remember scents and smells for a long time? Perhaps you recall the smell of a holiday beach or the house of a relative. Smell is one of the body's five main senses. The smell area inside the nose detects tiny invisible particles, called odour molecules, floating in the air. Smell checks whether our foods and drinks are not bad or rotten. It also warns us of danger, such as the nose-wrinkling smell of soft sinking mud, or the stench of stagnant, polluted water. Smell also gives pleasure, such as the lovely scents of flowers and perfumes, and the aromas of good food.

Enjoy the scents of beautiful blooms, like roses and carnations. Sniff each type of flower in turn, and ask your friends which scent they like best. People have different personal preferences for scents and smells.

Your nose runs or gets blocked when you have an infection by germs, such as a cold. Get rid of this nasal mucus by sneezing or blowing into a tissue or a handkerchief.

Inside the nose
The nostrils are separated by a dividing wall, the septum. They lead into a large hole called the nasal cavity. When you breathe in, air comes through the nostrils, passes through the nasal cavity, and goes down the back, to the throat and windpipe. The smell area is in the top of the nasal cavity, and it is about the size of your thumbnail.

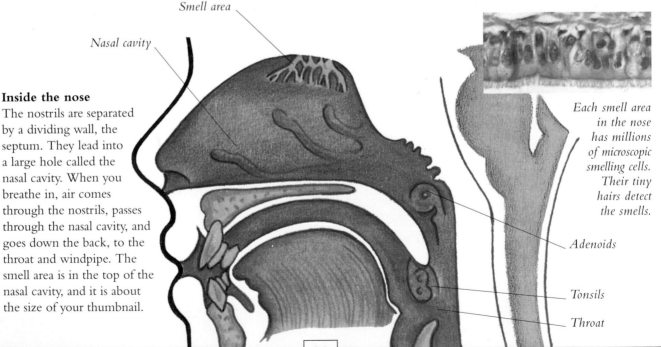

Smell area

Nasal cavity

Each smell area in the nose has millions of microscopic smelling cells. Their tiny hairs detect the smells.

Adenoids

Tonsils

Throat

A mouthwatering meal
Would you eat this well-prepared meal? Smell alone can make you hungry. Your brain recognizes food smells and gets your body ready. Watery saliva (spit) comes into your mouth, ready to moisten the chewing. This is why good food is said to smell "mouthwatering".

Bad and rotten!
Would you eat this old, rotting food? It looks awful, and if you could smell it, that would be even worse! If foods or drinks smell bad or rotten, they might cause food poisoning, so we avoid them. Smell gives us an early warning before we taste. This is a very important use of the sense of smell.

Overpowering fragrance
A few flowers are fine. But a whole field can be overpowering. Some smells are pleasant in normal amounts. But if they are too strong, they are not so nice. The amount or concentration of a smell alters its effects on us.

Sniff, sniff…
Is that smoke? This smell tells us immediately about the risk of danger. The body becomes alert and ready for action. Animals react in the same way to the smell of a forest or bush fire.

FACT BOX
• Most people could identify at least 10,000 different smells, if they had the time to try them all!

• A bloodhound sniffer-dog can smell things at least 1,000 times better than a person can.

• The smell areas inside the top of the nose have 20–30 million smelling cells.

TONGUE AND TASTE

As you eat your meal, you probably lick your lips slightly to clean them. This also moistens them, so they seal together well and stop food and drink dribbling out. Your tongue does many other jobs too. It provides you with your sense of taste by detecting tiny particles called flavour molecules in foods and drinks. Along with smell, taste helps to tell you if foods are sour, rotten or bad, and that you should not eat them. The tongue moves food around in your mouth, so you can chew it all properly. It also helps you to talk clearly, by moving around as you speak and make sounds.

Many animals use their tongues to clean their faces, whiskers, paws and other body parts. People do not need to, since we have hands, soap and water. But sometimes you might lick a stray bit of food or drink from your lips, or even your nose — if you can reach it!

Poking your tongue out is considered rude in some places, funny or friendly in others. Do it to yourself in a mirror. See the tongue's rough surface and the lumps (papillae).

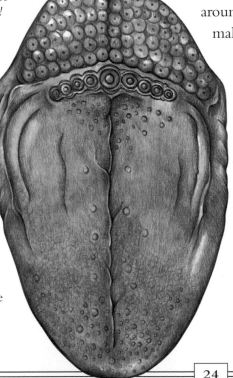

Bumpy tongue
The top surface of the tongue is covered with small lumps and bumps, called papillae. There are different kinds, with larger ones at the back. All the papillae help to grip and rub food as you bite and chew.

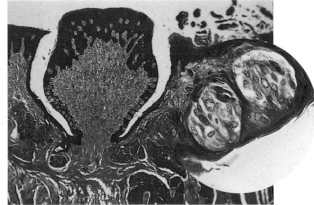

Taste buds
The microscope photograph, above left, shows a cut-through view of one papilla. Set into its lower edges (the stalk) are tiny taste buds. The enlarged view, above right, shows two taste buds with their tasting cells.

Tastes on the tongue

It is thought that there are five basic flavours – sweet, salty, savoury (also called umami), sour and bitter. All the varied tastes we experience, in foods and drinks, are made of different combinations of these basic tastes. They are detected over most parts of the tongue, especially the front tip, sides and rear. The upper middle of the tongue, and its underside, have very few taste buds and so hardly detect any flavours. There are also some taste buds on the roof of the mouth and in the upper throat.

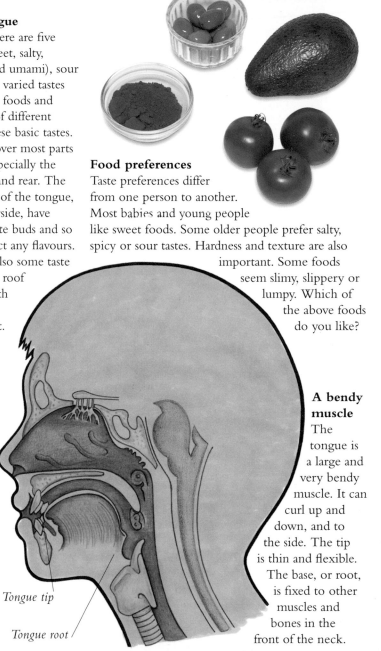

Food preferences

Taste preferences differ from one person to another. Most babies and young people like sweet foods. Some older people prefer salty, spicy or sour tastes. Hardness and texture are also important. Some foods seem slimy, slippery or lumpy. Which of the above foods do you like?

FACT BOX

• A typical tongue has more than 8,000 taste buds on it.

• Each taste bud has 20-30 "tasting cells" that identify what is in the mouth.

• The tasting cell in a taste bud only lives for 10 days, then it dies. But it is replaced within 12 hours by another one.

• Babies have more taste buds than adults, perhaps as many as 10,000.

• Older people usually have fewer taste buds, perhaps 5,000. So they may say that foods are bland and tasteless, while younger people with more taste buds disagree!

Tongue tip

Tongue root

A bendy muscle

The tongue is a large and very bendy muscle. It can curl up and down, and to the side. The tip is thin and flexible. The base, or root, is fixed to other muscles and bones in the front of the neck.

SMELL OR TASTE?

WHEN you eat and drink, you use the senses of taste, smell, touch and sight – all together! You detect tastes using the taste buds on your tongue. You detect smells which float from the back of your mouth, up into the back of your nose, as you chew. You assess the temperature, hardness, moistness and texture of food by the different types of touch sensors in your mouth. This is different from taste. You also look at the food with your eyes, to get an impression of how it might taste before you eat it. All four of these senses tell you about the smells and tastes of foods and drinks. But what happens if some of these senses are blocked off? Is it harder to tell what you're eating?

Some smells are similar. Sniff a spoonful of honey, then some jam. Can you tell the difference? They both smell sweet. Perhaps the jam has fruits in it, or the honey has real honeycomb in it.

You will need: small pots or jars with lids, cotton wool, adhesive labels, pencil, notebook, drinks and juices such as apple, orange, blackcurrant, tomato, pineapple, coffee, milk and tea.

Sniff test

1 Try the sniff test on your friends. Put a lump of cotton wool into some small jars. Label the jars A, B, etc. Make a list in your notebook of which juice or drink you will put into each jar. Keep the list secret!

2 Pour on to each lump of cotton wool the chosen drink or juice. Put on the lids. This stops the smells of each one escaping and mingling together in the air nearby, which could be confusing.

3 Ask your friends to take off the lids and sniff the jars, one by one, without looking inside. The only clue they have is smell. If the cotton wool is stained, ask your friends to wear a blindfold.

Taste test

Fading tastes

Why do the first few lollipop-licks always taste best? If you keep eating the same thing, its taste gradually fades. The flavour molecules are still there, but the tongue becomes less sensitive to them. The same happens with smells. This is called habituation.

MATERIALS

You will need: apple, banana, cheese, bread, pear, melon and similar pale and moist foods, table knife, blindfold.

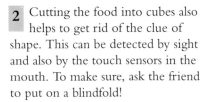

1 Try the taste test on your friends. Carefully peel each food and cut it into small cubes. Try to choose pale-looking foods, so there is little clue in the differences. This helps to remove information gained by sight.

2 Cutting the food into cubes also helps to get rid of the clue of shape. This can be detected by sight and also by the touch sensors in the mouth. To make sure, ask the friend to put on a blindfold!

3 When you have cubed all the foods, ask your friend to chew each one a few times, then swallow it. There are hardly any clues from smell or touch. Are the foods easy to identify by taste and texture alone?

NERVES AND BRAIN

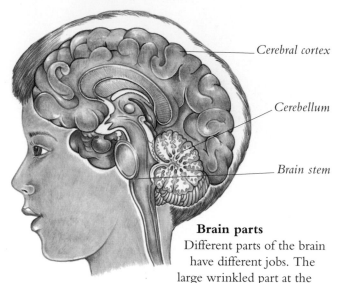

Cerebral cortex

Cerebellum

Brain stem

HAVE you used your brain today? Perhaps you have thought hard to solve a problem, or managed to remember something difficult. Thoughts, memories, ideas and wishes all happen in the brain. They are in the form of tiny electrical pulses, called nerve signals. These whizz about among the brain's complicated network of long, thin nerves – millions of them. Much more happens in the brain, too. It is where you feel emotions like love, fear and anger. It is where signals come to, from the senses. It is where you decide to make movements and actions. It is also the control box for all your body's inner processes, like heartbeat, breathing and digesting food. The brain is truly the body's central office, in control of the whole human.

Brain parts
Different parts of the brain have different jobs. The large wrinkled part at the top, the cerebral cortex, is where you think, remember, decide and become aware of what is happening. The cerebellum at the lower rear makes your movements smooth and coordinated. The lowest part, the brain stem, controls basic life processes like heartbeat.

Safe brain
The brain is very delicate. But it is well protected against knocks by the hard skull bone around it. Even so, it is always wise to wear a safety hat or helmet for extra protection, in case you get a bump on the head.

Seeing the brain
Medical scanners used in hospitals can see inside the head, without any pain or damage – and without cutting it open! They reveal any injury or disease. This enhanced photograph shows the wrinkled cerebral cortex and the two eyes with their optic nerves.

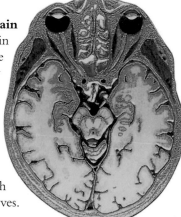

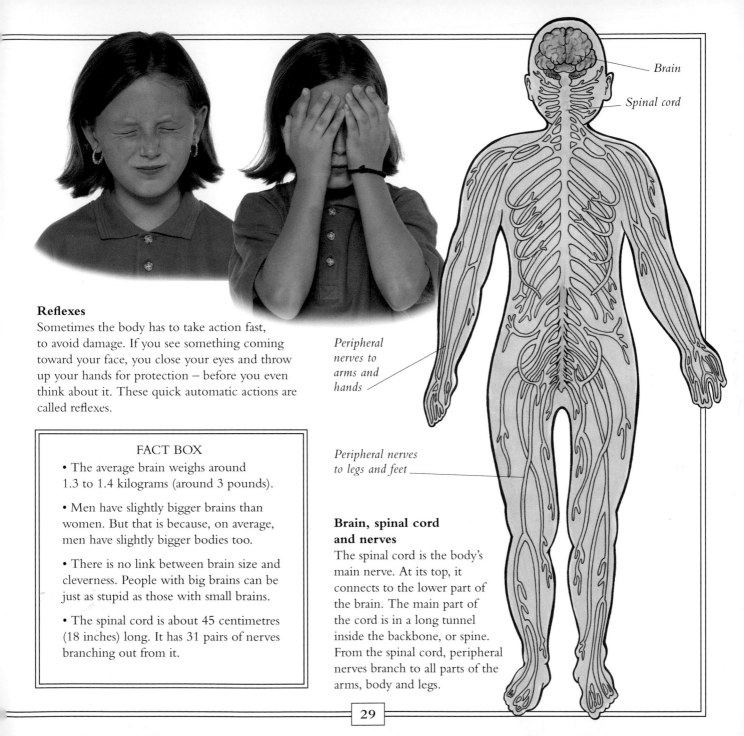

Brain

Spinal cord

Peripheral
nerves to
arms and
hands

Peripheral nerves
to legs and feet

Reflexes

Sometimes the body has to take action fast,
to avoid damage. If you see something coming
toward your face, you close your eyes and throw
up your hands for protection – before you even
think about it. These quick automatic actions are
called reflexes.

FACT BOX
• The average brain weighs around
1.3 to 1.4 kilograms (around 3 pounds).

• Men have slightly bigger brains than
women. But that is because, on average,
men have slightly bigger bodies too.

• There is no link between brain size and
cleverness. People with big brains can be
just as stupid as those with small brains.

• The spinal cord is about 45 centimetres
(18 inches) long. It has 31 pairs of nerves
branching out from it.

Brain, spinal cord and nerves

The spinal cord is the body's
main nerve. At its top, it
connects to the lower part of
the brain. The main part of
the cord is in a long tunnel
inside the backbone, or spine.
From the spinal cord, peripheral
nerves branch to all parts of the
arms, body and legs.

AWAKE AND ASLEEP

W HEN you wake up in the morning, and it feels as if you have had a good rest, most of your body has done. But some parts, like your heart and lungs, have been working all night. So has your brain. During sleep, it is busy doing various activities. No one knows exactly what, or why. But they must be important, because people who cannot sleep become confused, and suffer headaches and pains. They may even collapse.

When the brain and body need sleep, they tell you by feeling tired. If you ignore this, they go to sleep anyway. Young children can drop off to sleep almost anywhere!

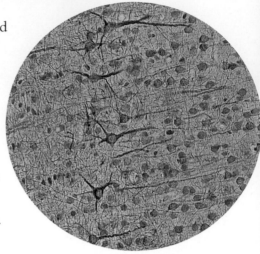

Nerve cells
Like other parts of the body, the brain and nerves are made of cells. They are called nerve cells or neurons. They have long, thin branches that connect to other nerve cells. There are more than 80 billion nerve cells in the brain, forming an immense network of pathways for nerve signals.

Brain areas
Different parts of the brain's outer surface, the cerebral cortex, deal with nerve signals coming from the senses. The signals from the eyes arrive at the seeing (visual) area, at the back. They are sorted and compared with patterns of signals already in the brain's memory. In this way, you recognize what you see. Other senses have similar areas.

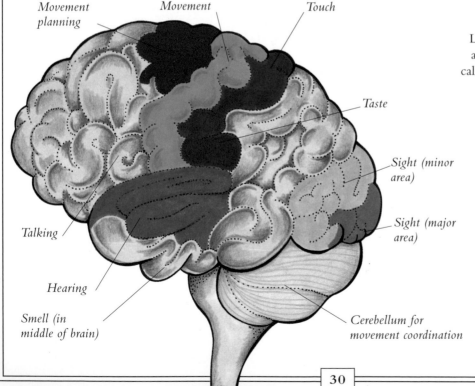

Movement planning

Movement

Touch

Taste

Sight (minor area)

Sight (major area)

Talking

Hearing

Smell (in middle of brain)

Cerebellum for movement coordination

The sides of the brain

The brain looks the same on each side. But the sides have different main activities. The left side takes charge in logic and reasoning, like solving problems in a step-by-step way, working with numbers, writing and speaking words. The right side tends to take the lead in creative and artistic processes like having new ideas, recognizing patterns, painting pictures and making music.

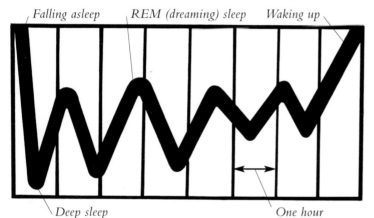

Falling asleep   *REM (dreaming) sleep*   *Waking up*

Deep sleep   *One hour*

Sleep and dreams

When you nod off each night, first you go into deep sleep. Body processes such as heartbeat and breathing slow down, and muscles relax. But after a time these processes speed up slightly. Muscles twitch and eyes flick about under closed lids. This is REM (rapid eye movement) sleep, when dreams usually happen. Then you go into deep sleep again, and so on, through the night.

Busy in bed

You do not stay completely still all night. Otherwise you would squash the nerves, blood vessels and other body parts you are lying on. You move and shift your position as many as 50 times.

FACT BOX
• A newborn baby needs about 20 hours of sleep each day.

• A 10-year-old needs about 10 hours' sleep each night.

• An adult needs seven to eight hours' sleep each night.

• But these are all averages. Some people have less sleep, others more. But whatever your sleep needs are, don't fight them.

MEMORIES

Some people write about their lives in a diary. This is a memory aid. They can look up a day which happened long ago. From a few words in the diary, they can begin to recall many other things that happened. The few words act as a memory trigger.

THERE is not one place in the brain for memories. They seem to be spread through several brain parts. Memories are probably complicated connections and pathways for nerve signals among the brain's millions of nerve cells. There are two stages to making a memory. One is to remember, which is to store the information in your brain. The other is to recall it, which is to find it again. You can play a sport or musical instrument better with practice – and you can do the same with memories. The more you try and learn to remember, the better you should become. There are also a few memory aids, short-cuts and "tricks" that you can use, as shown here.

MATERIALS

You will need for the memory tray: a selection of household toys, ornaments, utensils and similar small items.

Memory test

1 Lay out a row of about eight or ten small and everyday objects on a table. A friend looks at them for about 20 seconds. He or she tries to remember their names and their positions in the row.

2 The friend closes eyes, and you move two objects, to swap their positions. The friend then looks again, and tries to identify the moved items. This is usually easier than remembering all the items in order.

3 Study all the objects again and try to memorize them. One trick is to make a word from the first letter of each of their names. Or try to include their names in a silly story, to make them easier to recall.

Memories in smells and pictures

A picture or a smell triggers your memory by taking your mind back to where and when you saw what is in the picture or smelled the smell.

Picture memory game

Luck and judgement

Some games are partly luck. But you can usually play them better if you train yourself to remember certain things. You can work out where a card is in a sequence by remembering the cards before it.

1 Some people find that they can remember pictures better than numbers and words. Try this picture memory test. Look at pictures in a book for 20 seconds. Note their shapes and other details.

2 Now concentrate on the picture memories in your mind. Keep going through each part, so it stays "fresh". Repeat the details of the shapes and shading, and the names of any objects.

3 After another 20 seconds, close the book and describe the pictures or draw them. Get friends to try the same test. Do it several times. With practice, you should gradually become more skilled.

FOOD FOR THE BODY

I F you do not eat a meal for a few hours, you soon begin to feel hungry. This is your body's way of telling you that it needs more energy, to power its thousands of chemical life processes. And it needs more nutrients (raw materials) too, for running repairs, growth and body maintenance, so you eat. Food contains both energy and nutrients. Some animals eat only one kind of food. Pandas feed just on bamboo, and koalas munch solely on eucalyptus leaves. But the human body needs a wide variety of foods to stay healthy. In particular, fresh vegetables and fruits are very good for the body.

Imagine what you eat in a typical month. It probably adds up to about 50 kilograms (100 pounds) in weight of food, plus more than 100 litres (100 quarts) of drinks. Even more amazing, it turns into you!

Carbohydrates and fibre

Carbohydrates are the body's main energy source. They are found in rice, potatoes, bread and pasta. Fibre, also called roughage, is not fully digested, but it gives food bulk and texture, and it keeps the intestines working. Wholegrains (in muesli, for example), vegetables and fruit have plenty of fibre.

Protein and fat

Proteins provide raw materials for maintenance and growth. Proteins are found in meat, fish, dairy produce, and some vegetables such as peas and beans. Fats are needed in fairly small amounts for healthy nerves and other body parts.

Food gives you energy

The energy in foods is measured in kilojoules, symbol kJ. (An older unit is the calorie, short for kilocalorie, also written kcal. 4.2 kJ = 1 kcal.) For example, a slice of wholemeal bread contains about 250 kJ, plus useful vitamins, minerals and fibre. A bar of chocolate contains 1,000 kJ, but little else. Your energy needs depend mainly on how active you are. If you eat too much high-energy food, such as biscuits or chips, the body converts them to fat.

Standing still or resting uses about 4 kJ per minute.

Walking or gentle activity uses 12 kJ per minute.

Running or hard exercise uses 30 kJ per minute.

Fruit

Most fruits, such as passionfruit and strawberries, are a good source of sugars, for energy, as well as providing vitamins, minerals and fibre.

Vegetables

You need to eat lots of vegetables every day, for the energy, fibre, vitamins and minerals they provide. Dark green vegetables are especially good for you.

The body contains an amazing assortment of minerals and substances, including iron (as in nails) and sulphur (as in match-heads). And the human body is three-fifths water!

MOUTH AND TEETH

THE first stop for the body's food is its mouth, with its various parts – lips, teeth, tongue and cheeks. Each part has a job to do. The teeth bite off pieces of food, and chew and squash and mash them. The lips open to let the food in, then seal together so that it does not fall out. The cheeks bulge as the tongue moves the food around between the teeth, for thorough chewing. As food is chewed, it is mixed with watery saliva or spit, to make it soft and moist. Then the tongue pushes the squidgy, mashed lump of food back into the throat, for swallowing down into the stomach. All of the mouth's chewing work helps us to digest food.

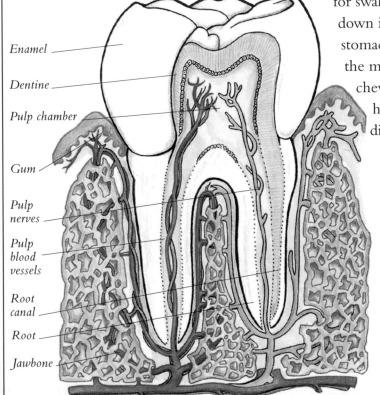

Enamel

Dentine

Pulp chamber

Gum

Pulp nerves

Pulp blood vessels

Root canal

Root

Jawbone

If an item of food is too big for your mouth, you can try to break it with your fingers, or cut it up with a knife. The easiest way is usually to bite off a piece, using your sharp front teeth, the incisors.

Inside a tooth

A tooth's upper part, the crown, is covered by whitish enamel, the hardest substance in the body. Underneath is dentine, slightly softer to absorb knocks and great pressure. The tooth's lower part, the root, anchors it in the jawbone. In the middle is a living pulp of blood vessels to provide nourishment, and nerves that warn of too much pressure, or dental decay – toothache! Clean your teeth morning and night, after every meal if possible, to remove the leftover food and germs that cause tooth decay. Visit the dentist regularly for a check on teeth and gums, and for advice on cleaning and flossing teeth.

Enamel

This cross-section of a tooth, magnified 275 times, shows that tooth enamel is formed from thousands of tiny rods.

Diets of the dead

We can tell what people have eaten, even after they die, from the shapes of their teeth, and the tiny marks and scratches on the tooth surface. These clues show that prehistoric people such as "Heidelberg Man", who lived perhaps half a million years ago, ate plenty of tough plant roots and shoots.

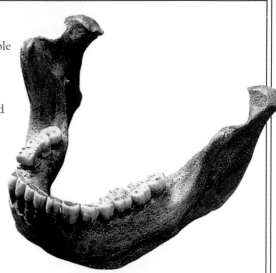

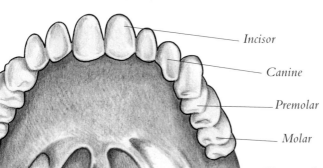

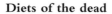 — *Incisor*

 — *Canine*

— *Premolar*

— *Molar*

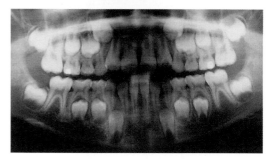

Types of teeth

The four main kinds of teeth are shaped to do different jobs. Incisors at the front are wide and sharp-edged like chisels, for biting and nibbling. Canines are longer and more pointed, to tear and rip. Premolars and molars at the back are broad and fairly flat, to squash and crush.

Hidden teeth

A dental X-ray shows a child's adult teeth under their milk teeth. From about the age of six, the milk teeth fall out and are replaced by the adult or permanent teeth. In each half of each jaw (upper and lower) a child has 2 incisors, 1 canine and 2 molars, making a total of 20 teeth. An adult has 2 incisors, 1 canine, 2 premolars and 3 molars, making a total of 32 teeth.

THE DIGESTIVE SYSTEM

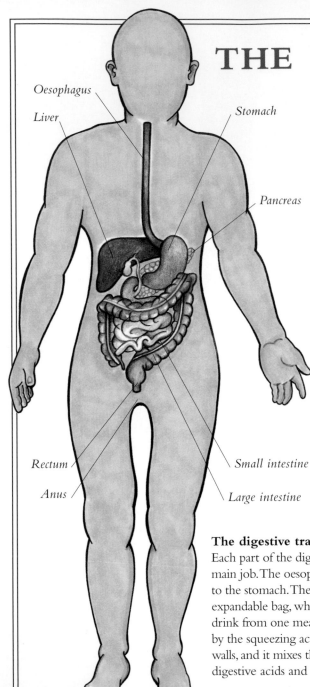

Oesophagus

Liver

Stomach

Pancreas

Rectum

Anus

Small intestine

Large intestine

SWALLOWED food starts a journey of about 9 metres (10 yards) and 24 hours long, through the body's digestive tract. This is like a long tube that starts at the mouth and finishes at the anus. Some parts of the tube, such as the stomach, are wider than others. Some parts, such as the small intestine, are folded and coiled to fit into the lower body. The digestive tract breaks down or digests swallowed food by squashing and mashing it, and adding powerful chemicals called acids and enzymes. Finally the digested bits of food become so small that they are molecules. They can pass through the tube lining into the body itself. These digested nutrients are carried away by the blood, which distributes them to all body parts.

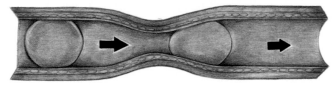

Food moves through the digestive tract by the action of muscles in the tract's walls. They contract in waves to squeeze and push the food along. This is called peristalsis, and it happens throughout the digestive tract, from oesophagus to rectum.

The digestive tract

Each part of the digestive system has its main job. The oesophagus carries food to the stomach. The stomach is an expandable bag, which holds food and drink from one meal. It pulps the food by the squeezing actions of muscles in its walls, and it mixes the food with powerful digestive acids and enzymes. The small intestine adds more enzymes to the soupy food, and absorbs the digested nutrients into the blood flowing through its wall. The large intestine or colon absorbs fluids, salts and minerals to leave semi-solid leftovers, also known as faeces. The rectum stores faeces until the body pushes them out through the muscular ring of the anus.

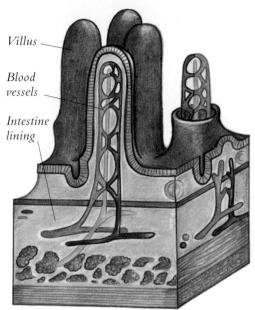

Villus

Blood vessels

Intestine lining

Inside the intestine

The small intestine lining has thousands of tiny short hair-like parts, called villi. These give a large surface area for absorbing food. Each villus has blood vessels that carry the digested food away to where it is needed.

Parts of the system

The liver and pancreas are not part of the digestive tract, but they are part of the digestive system. The liver receives blood from the small intestine, loaded with nutrients. It processes, stores, alters and distributes them according to the body's needs. The pancreas makes digestive enzymes that pour into the small intestine, to help food break down.

Digestion times

The amount of time it takes for food to travel through your digestive system varies, depending on how easy it is to digest.

Digestive juices

Tiny pits in the lining of the stomach (*above*) and between the villi of the small intestine ooze digestive juices. These consist of enzymes and powerful acids which break down the food.

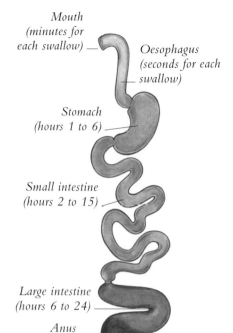

Mouth (minutes for each swallow)

Oesophagus (seconds for each swallow)

Stomach (hours 1 to 6)

Small intestine (hours 2 to 15)

Large intestine (hours 6 to 24)

Anus (hours 12 to 24)

FACT BOX

• The oesophagus is about 25 centimetres (10 inches) long and 2–3 centimetres (1 inch) wide. Its walls are very muscular.

• The stomach can expand to hold more than 1.5 litres (1½ quarts) of foods and fluids.

• The small intestine is 6 metres (20 feet) long and 2–3 centimetres (1 inch) wide.

• The large intestine is 1.5 metres (5 feet) long and about 5 centimetres (2 inches) wide.

• The rectum is 15 centimetres (6 inches) long and about 5 centimetres (2 inches) wide.

EATING AND DRINKING

Many important events include a meal, from the cake and ice-cream of a birthday party, to the many courses of a huge banquet when meeting kings or presidents.

FOOD provides fuel for the body, and much more. It gives us great enjoyment and pleasure, as we eat a delicious meal. For some people, cooking food is a skilled job, or an interesting pastime – or even an obsession! Food also gives us the opportunity to take a break and meet others. When we sit down for a meal, we have time to pause from the rush of the day, think and consider what to do next. We can appreciate the meal and drinks, and chat and spend time with family and friends. Trying to eat while moving about or doing other things can cause problems. We may not chew thoroughly, and rushed food may even choke us.

You will need: dry crackers or similar dry biscuits or cookies (plus a drink).

Make your mouth water

A moist mouth

Watery saliva, or spit, is made in three pairs of salivary glands around the face. Saliva softens and moistens food as you chew, so that you can mash it to a squishy pulp and swallow it more easily. It also begins the chemical breakdown (digestion) of the starch in food. Normally we do not notice saliva and what it does, since many foods are moist. But if you eat very dry foods, you soon notice its lack!

1 Bite off and chew a piece of cracker. Chew slowly. Can you feel the saliva making the dry cracker damp and soft? Swallow, and eat another piece.

2 And eat some more. The salivary glands make about 1 litre of saliva daily. But there is only a limited amount in a few minutes, less than 100 millilitres (4 ounces).

3 How many crackers can you eat, before they become too dry and hard to chew? Your saliva is used up, and you need a drink to finish the job.

Strange-looking foods

Before we eat, we check that a meal is safe to eat. We sniff for its smell, and we look at it to identify the foods. Are they the right shape and shade? If these appear odd, such as purple carrots instead of orange, we might be worried about eating them. This is a natural reaction or instinct. Blue foods, such as this blue pasta, look especially odd. Can you think of more than two or three natural, safe blue foods?

Funny texture

The appearance of food in terms of texture is important too. Breaded fish, fried eggs and vegetables normally look tasty, but if you mash them up you probably will not want them any more!

You will need: selection of foods, such as bread, weighing scales, supervised use of an oven.

The body needs about 2 litres (2 quarts) or more of water every day. Some of this comes in as foods, the rest as drinks. How much of a food is water?

Water in food

1 Carefully weigh the chosen piece of food, such as a slice of bread. Ask an adult to put the food in a suitable container in the oven, next time this is on.

2 Heat the food until it is dry, but not burned. Let the container and food cool. Remove the food and weigh it again. What proportion was water, now evaporated?

BODY WASTES

ALL animals produce wastes, from small mouse droppings to huge mounds of elephant dung. The human body does, too. Like cats, dogs and similar creatures, it makes two main kinds of wastes. There are solid wastes, also called faeces or bowel movements (and many other names!), and liquid wastes, also known as urine or "water" (and many other names!). These two kinds of wastes have very different origins. Faeces are the leftovers at the end of the digestive process. They come out of the end of the digestive tract. Urine is mainly made up of chemical wastes and excess water filtered from the blood, by the parts called the kidneys. It comes from the bladder. The body also produces a waste gas called carbon dioxide, which it breathes out through the lungs.

MATERIALS

You will need: large and small plastic funnels, adhesive tape.

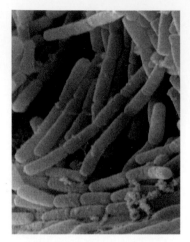

Not all microbes are harmful germs. These friendly bacteria live in everyone's intestines, and they help with digestion.

Listen to your tummy

1 You can hear wastes gurgling through the digestive system, with two funnels. Push the spouts of the two funnels together tightly.

2 Tape the spouts together. The large funnel acts as a sound-collector for body noises such as digestion or heartbeat.

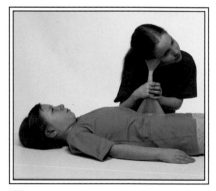

3 Press the large funnel on to a friend's abdomen, and the small one around your ear. Can you hear food slurping and gases bubbling?

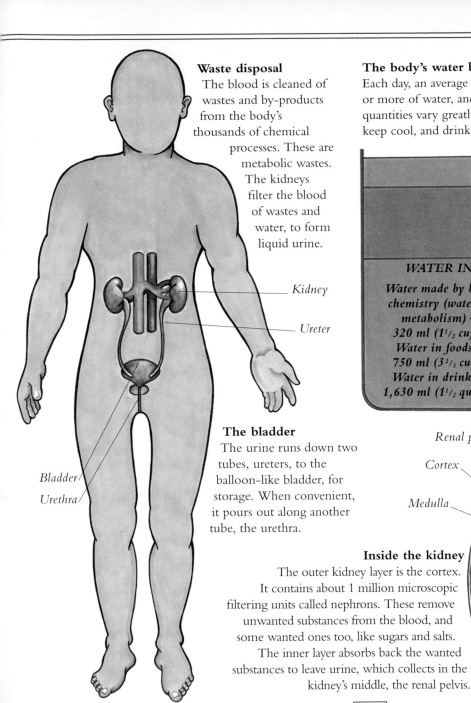

Waste disposal

The blood is cleaned of wastes and by-products from the body's thousands of chemical processes. These are metabolic wastes. The kidneys filter the blood of wastes and water, to form liquid urine.

Kidney

Ureter

Bladder
Urethra

The bladder

The urine runs down two tubes, ureters, to the balloon-like bladder, for storage. When convenient, it pours out along another tube, the urethra.

The body's water balance

Each day, an average body takes in about 2.5 litres (3 quarts) or more of water, and gives out the same amount. But these quantities vary greatly. In hot weather, you sweat more to keep cool, and drink more to replace this perspired water.

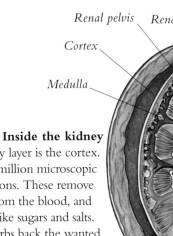

WATER IN

Water made by body chemistry (water of metabolism) – 320 ml (1½ cups)
Water in foods – 750 ml (3⅔ cups)
Water in drinks – 1,630 ml (1½ quarts)

WATER OUT

Water in faeces – 100 ml (½ cup)
Water in urine – 1,760 ml (1½ quarts)
Water in sweat and as vapour in breathed-out air – 840 ml (3¾ cups)

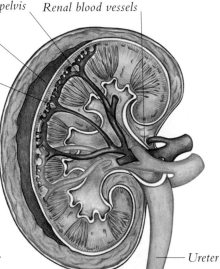

Renal pelvis   *Renal blood vessels*

Cortex

Medulla

Ureter

Inside the kidney

The outer kidney layer is the cortex. It contains about 1 million microscopic filtering units called nephrons. These remove unwanted substances from the blood, and some wanted ones too, like sugars and salts. The inner layer absorbs back the wanted substances to leave urine, which collects in the kidney's middle, the renal pelvis.

LUNGS AND BREATHING

ALL animals and plants need oxygen for life. Oxygen is an invisible gas in the air around us. It is required for part of the chemical changes that happen in every body cell, to break down digested foods and nutrients, and get the energy from them. This energy powers muscles and the body's life processes. The series of chemical changes is called aerobic respiration. The body cannot store oxygen, so it must get fresh supplies every minute. It does this by breathing (respiring). The parts involved in breathing and absorbing oxygen from the air are called the respiratory system. They include the nose, throat, windpipe (trachea) and the two spongy, cone-shaped lungs in the chest.

The two lungs normally hold about 2.5 litres (13 cubic feet) of air. But when the body is very active it needs more oxygen for its busy muscles. If you breathe in deeply, the lungs hold over 5 litres (25 cubic feet) of air.

Well-trained humans can hold their breath for a minute or so when swimming underwater. But for longer periods, we need to take our own oxygen supply with us to breathe. This is contained as pressurized air or oxygen mixture inside scuba tanks.

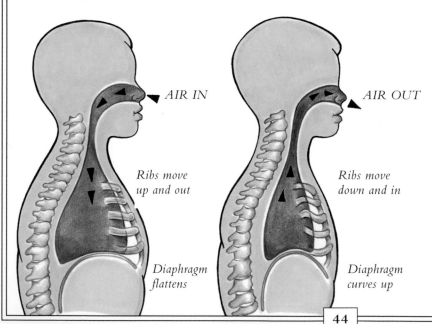

AIR IN

Ribs move up and out

Diaphragm flattens

AIR OUT

Ribs move down and in

Diaphragm curves up

Muscles for breathing

The movements of breathing are called bodily respiration. They are made by two main sets of muscles. One is the diaphragm, a sheet of muscle under the lungs. The other set is the intercostals, short muscles between each pair of ribs.

In and out

To breathe in, the diaphragm contracts to become shorter and flatter, and the lungs stretch downwards. The intercostals contract, pulling up the ribs, which stretches the lungs forwards. The stretched lungs suck in air. To breathe out, the diaphragm and intercostals relax. The stretched lungs spring back, and blow out air.

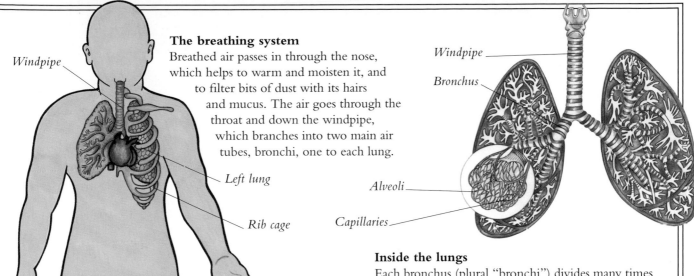

The breathing system
Breathed air passes in through the nose, which helps to warm and moisten it, and to filter bits of dust with its hairs and mucus. The air goes through the throat and down the windpipe, which branches into two main air tubes, bronchi, one to each lung.

Windpipe

Left lung

Rib cage

Windpipe

Bronchus

Alveoli

Capillaries

Fair exchange
Breathing not only takes oxygen into the body. It also gets rid of carbon dioxide, a waste product made in cells by aerobic respiration. This is collected by the blood and passes into the air in the lungs, for breathing out. If carbon dioxide built up in the blood, it would soon poison the body.

Inside the lungs
Each bronchus (plural "bronchi") divides many times into smaller air tubes, bronchioles. These end in about 250 million microscopic air bubbles, called alveoli, surrounded by networks of microscopic blood vessels, capillaries. Oxygen from air in the alveoli seeps the very short distance to the blood in the capillaries, to be pumped around the body.

FACT BOX
• At rest, an average person breathes in and out about 14–16 times each minute.

• After lots of exercise, this can rise to more than 60 times each minute.

• At rest, an average person breathes in and out about 0.5 litres (30 cubic inches) of air.

• After lots of exercise, this can rise to more than 2 litres (10 cubic feet) of air with each breath.

• At rest, new babies breathe about 40-50 times each minute, much faster than adults. This slows to 25 times each minute by the age of 5 years.

BREATHED-IN AIR
Nitrogen – 78 per cent
Oxygen – 21 per cent
Carbon dioxide – 0.04 per cent
Plus other gases

BREATHED-OUT AIR
Nitrogen – 79 per cent
Oxygen – 16 per cent
Carbon dioxide – 4 per cent
Plus other gases

BREATHING AND BLOWING

Breathing has many uses, in addition to obtaining oxygen. As the moving air passes through your voice-box or larynx in your neck, it allows you to talk and sing. If you purse your lips or blow through a narrow gap between your fingers, you can whistle. If you blow out hard, you can spin toy windmills and inflate balloons. When you blow out forcefully like this, you use extra muscles in your abdomen and chest. Breathing also works many musical instruments, from recorders to trumpets and tubas.

Hold a toy windmill in front of your mouth and breathe normally. Does it spin? Blow gently, then hard. Does it move? Try different breathing-type actions such as talking, shouting and whistling. Which spins the windmill fastest?

Don't blow too hard

As you blow up a balloon, you force air from your lungs up your windpipe and mouth, into the balloon. But this requires lots of muscle power in your chest and abdomen, and great air pressure in your lungs. If you try too hard for too long, it could damage the lungs' delicate air bubbles (alveoli) that take in oxygen. A proper air pump for blowing up balloons is much less risky!

How fast do you breathe?

Find out using a stopwatch or similar timepiece, to time your breaths. Breathing in, then out, is one breath. Count the number of breaths in 30 seconds and double it to find the rate per minute. Try various activities and see how they affect your breathing rate.

Sit at rest for 5 minutes and count your breaths. How do you compare with the average rates on the previous page? Next, say your favourite nursery rhyme several times, and count your breathing rate as you do this. (Talking as you breathe out is the out-breath.) Then run on the spot for 5 minutes, and count the rate again. How fast does it get?

M A T E R I A L S

You will need: water, large shallow bowl, large glass or clear plastic see-through jar or measuring cup, length of tubing or garden hose or similar flexible pipe.

The breath machine

You can compare the amounts of air you breathe when doing different actions, using this home-made version of the scientific device called a spirometer. You breathe out air through the tube, and it bubbles into the water-filled jar and pushes the water out. The lower the water level in the jar after the breath, the bigger the volume of that breath.

Water level in jar showing volume of breathed-out air.

4 After breathing in from the air, breathe out carefully into the tube.

Warning
Never breathe in through the tube, or you could cough and choke on water!

How much air?

1 Half-fill the large shallow bowl with water and put it on a firm surface. Also, completely fill the large jar with water.

2 Place the tube into the water, ready to place the jar on top. With your hand sealed over the jar's mouth, quickly turn it upside down.

3 Put the jar in the bowl, take your hand away and the water should stay in the jar. Put one end of the tube under the rim, into the jar.

TALKING

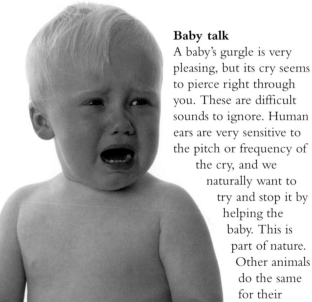

Birds such as parrots and mynahs can imitate many sounds, from the noise of a car or telephone, to words of human speech. But the bird does not understand or mean what it says.

HAVE you been told off for talking too much? In fact, who hasn't? Too much chat is sometimes out of place. But speech is a natural, everyday part of life. Humans are generally social creatures and like to be in groups with family and friends. Speech is our main form of communication. We talk about foods and drinks, sports and the weather, wishes and wants, and how we think and feel. The sounds of speech are made possible by the vocal cords in the larynx (voice-box), which is in the neck. This is part of the respiratory system (the lungs and the windpipe). We also communicate by making facial expressions such as smiles and frowns, by using our hands, and by our general body posture, actions and movements. This is called body language. In the right situation, a small yet silent movement of part of the body can say more than words ever could.

Baby talk
A baby's gurgle is very pleasing, but its cry seems to pierce right through you. These are difficult sounds to ignore. Human ears are very sensitive to the pitch or frequency of the cry, and we naturally want to try and stop it by helping the baby. This is part of nature. Other animals do the same for their offspring.

Meaning without talking
The vocal cords make many other vocal sounds, besides speech. We laugh, cry, sob and hum. These and many other sounds made by the cords are called vocalizations. They also convey messages such as happiness or sadness. The loudness and other features of the sound are also important. A loud, short shout usually means a warning or attracts attention. Whispering sweet nothings shows affection!

Shaping the sounds

The vibrations from the vocal cords themselves are surprisingly quiet and indistinct. We make them into clear words and other vocal sounds using the mouth, lips, teeth, tongue and cheeks. Look in a mirror and see how these parts move as you make different sounds, such as f, m, o, e and l.

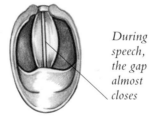

Vocal cord

Gap between cords

During speech, the gap almost closes

Inside the voice-box

Vocal sounds come from the larynx, at the top of the windpipe. This has two flaps or folds that stick out from its sides, called vocal cords. There is a wide gap between them, the glottis, for normal breathing. To speak, laryngeal muscles pull the cords almost together, so there is hardly any gap between them. Air flows past and makes them vibrate to produce sounds. The tighter they stretch, the higher the sound.

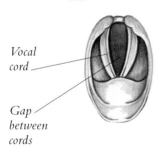

Louder and louder

In some places, like a crowded concert hall, the human voice is not loud enough. So we make it louder using electrical power. The microphone works like a human ear, changing the voice's sound waves into tiny pulses of electricity. An amplifier makes these much stronger. The pulses feed into a loudspeaker, which works in the same way as the vocal cords. It vibrates to reproduce the sound waves, but much more loudly.

BLOOD AND ITS TUBES

To stay alive, all the cells in the body need continuing supplies of oxygen, energy and nutrients. And they all produce waste substances that must be removed. The blood is the body's transport system – its delivery and collection service. Blood brings oxygen from the lungs, and raw materials, such as energy-rich sugars and other nutrients from digestion, for use by cells. It collects carbon dioxide for removal by the lungs, and wastes to be filtered by the kidneys. Blood manages to do this because it flows around every part and corner of the body in a vast network of branching tubes, called blood vessels. It flows because it is pumped by regular contractions of a hollow bag of muscle – the heart. The heart, blood vessels and blood are called the circulatory system.

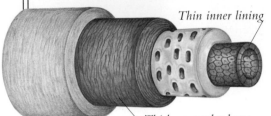

Thin inner lining

Thick, muscular layer

Arteries

These blood vessels carry blood away from the heart. They have thick, elastic walls to withstand the high pressure of blood as it surges from the heart with each beat. They divide many times, becoming smaller until they form capillaries.

Wall one cell thick

Capillaries

Capillaries are less than 1 millimetre (four-hundredths of an inch) long and are far too thin to see. Oxygen, nutrients and other substances seep through their walls, to the cells beyond. Capillaries join to make veins.

Veins

Veins carry blood back to the heart. They are thin-walled and floppy, since blood has lost most of its surging pressure after passing through the microscopic capillaries.

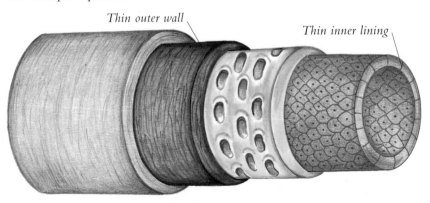

Thin outer wall

Thin inner lining

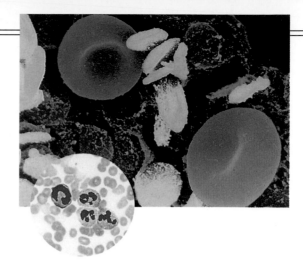

The blood system

The network of arteries, capillaries and veins spreads through the entire body, even into bones and muscles. The large blood vessels have individual names and are in much the same place in each human body. The smaller ones vary from one person to another.

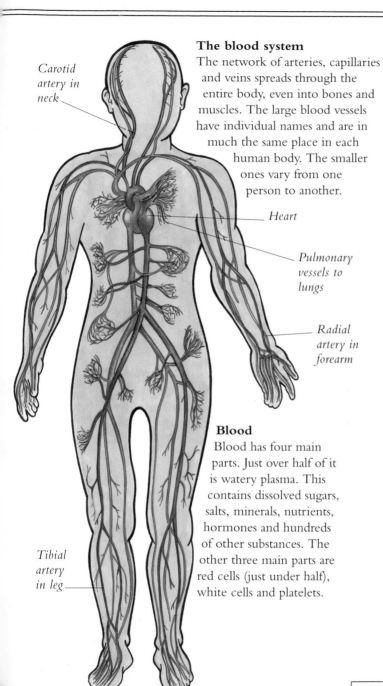

Carotid artery in neck

Heart

Pulmonary vessels to lungs

Radial artery in forearm

Tibial artery in leg

Blood

Blood has four main parts. Just over half of it is watery plasma. This contains dissolved sugars, salts, minerals, nutrients, hormones and hundreds of other substances. The other three main parts are red cells (just under half), white cells and platelets.

Blood cells

Blood contains millions of cells. Red blood cells (shown in red in the top picture) carry oxygen. They pick it up in the capillaries in the lungs, and release it to the cells all around the body. Platelets (shown in yellow in the top picture) help blood to clot, to seal a cut or a wound. White blood cells (in the circle) clean the blood and body tissues, and fight germs. They can surround and "eat" germs, dead cells and other debris.

FACT BOX

• An average adult body has about 5 litres (5 quarts) of blood.

• At any moment three-quarters of the blood is in the veins, one-fifth in the arteries, and the remaining one-twentieth in the capillaries.

• If all the blood vessels in the body were joined end to end, they would stretch 100,000 kilometres (62,000 miles), which is two and a half times around the Earth.

HEART AND HEARTBEAT

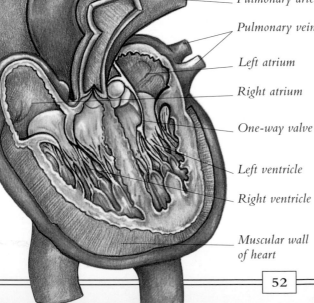

THE beating heart is the symbol of life. If the heart stops pumping, blood stops flowing. The blood can no longer deliver nutrients, and especially oxygen, around the body. Without oxygen, and with wastes building up, cells begin to die within minutes. The heart is like a hollow bag with very strong, muscular walls. As the muscles contract, they squeeze blood inside the heart out into the arteries. As the muscles relax, more blood flows into the heart from the veins. The heart's thick walls are made from a specialized type of muscle, called cardiac muscle. It never tires.

...lub-dub, lub-dub...

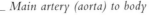

Main artery (aorta) to body

Pulmonary arteries to lungs

Pulmonary veins from lungs

Left atrium

Right atrium

One-way valve

Left ventricle

Right ventricle

Muscular wall of heart

The heart is between the lungs in the middle of the chest, slightly to the left side, protected by the breastbone and ribs. It is about the size of its owner's clenched fist.

Inside the heart

The heart is not one pump, but two. Each pump has a small upper chamber, the atrium (plural "atria"), and a large lower one, the ventricle. One-way valves inside the heart make blood flow the correct way (from the atrium to the ventricle and then into the arteries), rather than simply sloshing to and fro with each heartbeat.

52

The stages of a heartbeat

The heartbeat is one smooth and continuous process, but it can be shown in stages to see what happens.

1 Blood flows from the main veins into the small upper chambers on each side, the atria.

2 The atria squeeze blood through one-way valves into the lower chambers, the ventricles. These have much thicker muscle walls.

3 The ventricles fill with blood and their muscular walls begin to contract powerfully.

4 Blood is forced at high pressure through more one-way valves, from the ventricles out into the main arteries.

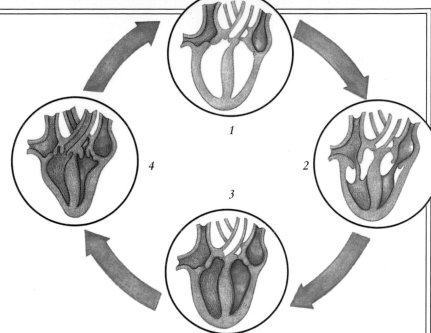

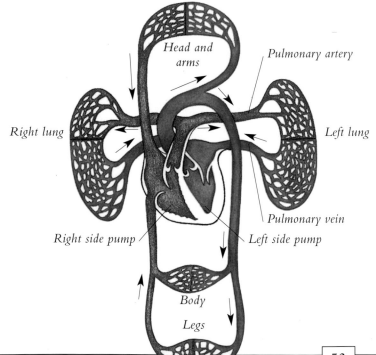

Blood around the body

Blood flows around the body's circulation in two stages. It leaves the heart's left side and goes into the branching arteries, capillaries and veins of the main body, head, arms and legs. This is the systemic circulation, delivering oxygen and nutrients to body cells.

Blood to the lungs

After going round the body, low-oxygen blood goes into the heart's right side. It is then pumped to the lungs in the pulmonary arteries, to pick up more oxygen and become bright red. This is the pulmonary circulation. Blood then goes back to the heart's left side to be pumped on to travel around the body. And the journey continues, in a never-ending, continuous flow. An average trip around the systemic and pulmonary circulations takes one minute.

PULSE

Each time the heart beats, it sends a surge of pressurized blood into the body's arteries. The pressure makes the elastic artery walls bulge outwards. This happens as bulges in all the arteries, spreading out from the heart. The pulsations or bulges are easiest to feel in arteries that are near the surface of the body, just under the skin. They are called the pulse, and there is one pulsation for each heartbeat. So counting the pulse rate is the same as counting the heartbeat rate. When the body is active or excited, the pulse rate goes up. This means the heart is beating faster, to send more energy and oxygen in the blood to the muscles, so that they can be active. Heart rate is under the control of nerve signals from the brain. It is also affected by adrenaline – one of the chemicals called hormones which control many body processes.

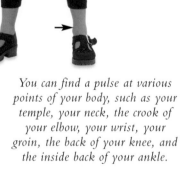

You can find a pulse at various points of your body, such as your temple, your neck, the crook of your elbow, your wrist, your groin, the back of your knee, and the inside back of your ankle.

Finding the pulse

Put two fingers on the inside of the wrist, just below the mound of the lower thumb. Do not use your own thumb, since it has a fairly strong pulse of its own. Press gently and feel for the pulsating artery, in the hollow next to the hard cord-like tendons in the wrist. Count the number of pulses in 1 minute.

How the pulse rate varies

Changes in pulse rate with exercise can indicate the body's general fitness. Measure your pulse rate at rest, every minute after walking for 5 minutes, and every minute after running for 2 minutes. The time taken for the rate to return to normal is called the recovery time. Usually, the shorter it is, the better.

You will need: drinking straw, scissors, reusable adhesive, stopwatch or clock.

See your pulse

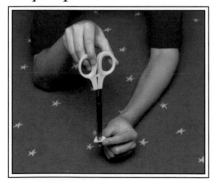

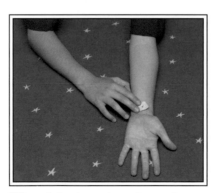

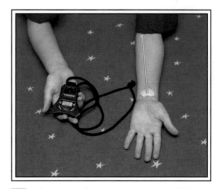

1 You can see the pulse rather than feeling it, with this simple pulse-meter. Carefully make a hole in a small blob of reusable adhesive.

2 Feel for the wrist pulse, as shown opposite. Press the blob firmly on the spot, without flattening it. Push the straw into the hole.

3 The tiny skin movements of the pulse are enlarged along the straw. Time the pulse as the straw tip flicks from side to side.

BONES AND JOINTS

Most parts of the human body are soft and floppy. Nerves, veins and intestines could not stand up by themselves. So the body has an inner framework to give it shape and support. It is called the skeleton, and it is made of 206 bones. A bone is not white, brittle, flaky and dead, like bones in museum cases. Inside the body, bones are very much alive. They are pale grey, and strong and tough. A bone is stiff but slightly flexible, so it usually bends under strain, rather than snapping. Like other body parts, a bone is made by cells and contains cells. It has its own nerves, blood vessels and other supplies. Bones are linked together at joints, so that they can move when they are pulled by muscles.

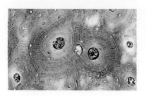

This microscope view of the inside of a bone shows that it is made of hundreds of tiny rods packed together. In the middle of each rod are miniature blood vessels.

Like joints, knees and elbows work like an ordinary hinge. The spine is like a string of beads, with the spinal column running down the middle.

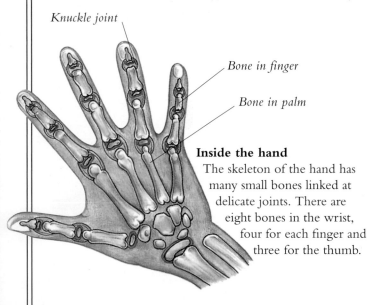

Knuckle joint

Bone in finger

Bone in palm

Inside the hand
The skeleton of the hand has many small bones linked at delicate joints. There are eight bones in the wrist, four for each finger and three for the thumb.

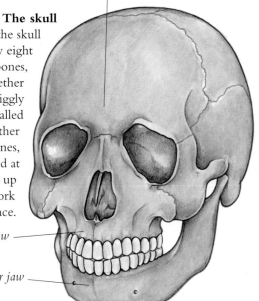

Frontal bone forms the forehead

The skull
The dome of the skull is formed by eight large curved bones, fixed together firmly at wiggly joint lines called sutures. Another 13 small bones, also joined at sutures, make up the framework of the face.

Upper jaw

Lower jaw

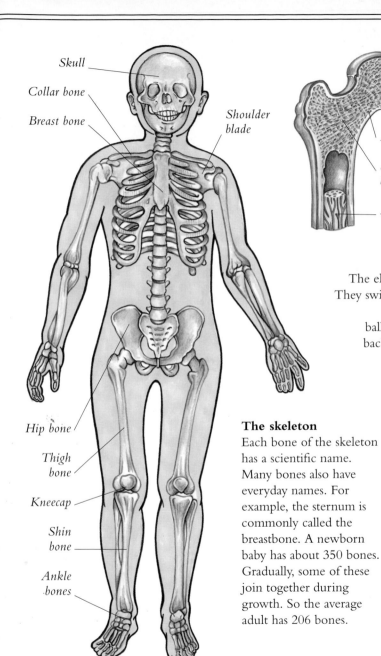

Skull

Collar bone

Breast bone

Shoulder blade

Hip bone

Thigh bone

Kneecap

Shin bone

Ankle bones

Inside a bone
Most bones have a tough, dense, strong outer layer made of compact or hard bone. Inside is a slightly softer, lighter type of bone, called spongy bone. Inside this is a space filled with jelly-like bone marrow, which makes new cells for the blood.

Hard bone

Spongy bone

Marrow

Shoulder

Elbow

Types of joints
The elbow and knee are hinge joints. They swing backward and forward only. The shoulder and hip are ball-and-socket joints. They move backward, forward and to the side. They also allow some twisting.

The skeleton
Each bone of the skeleton has a scientific name. Many bones also have everyday names. For example, the sternum is commonly called the breastbone. A newborn baby has about 350 bones. Gradually, some of these join together during growth. So the average adult has 206 bones.

FACT BOX

• Bones are made of two main substances. One is collagen, a body protein, also found in skin. It makes the bone slightly flexible.

• The other substances are mineral crystals, especially calcium and phosphates. These give bone its hardness and toughness.

• The body's biggest bone is the femur (the thigh bone). The smallest bone is the tiny stirrup, deep in the ear.

• Where bones meet in a joint, they are covered with cartilage. This is shiny and slippery, for smooth movements and to prevent the bone ends from wearing away.

MUSCLES

Bones give the body a strong inner framework, and the joints between them allow the bones to bend and straighten. But without the skeletal muscles to pull the bones, the body could not move. Without the cardiac muscles in the walls of the heart, the blood would not go round the body. Without the muscles in the walls of the oesophagus, stomach and intestines, the body could not push food through its digestive system. Muscles make every movement of the body happen. This includes inner processes such as digestion and circulation, and body actions such as walking and running.

Hundreds of muscles work together as teams to make the body do amazing and complex actions, from playing tennis to playing a musical instrument.

About 40 facial muscles make expressions of all kinds, especially a wide smile!

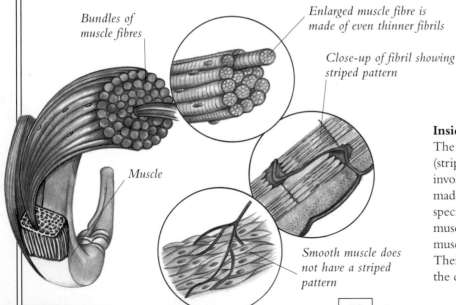

Bundles of muscle fibres

Enlarged muscle fibre is made of even thinner fibrils

Close-up of fibril showing striped pattern

Muscle

Smooth muscle does not have a striped pattern

Inside muscle
The three main types of muscles are skeletal (striped or voluntary), visceral (smooth or involuntary) and cardiac (heart). They are all made from groups of large cells which are specialized to contract (get shorter). Skeletal muscles are bundles of huge cells called muscle fibres, almost as thick as hairs. Their movements are voluntary (under the conscious control of your brain).

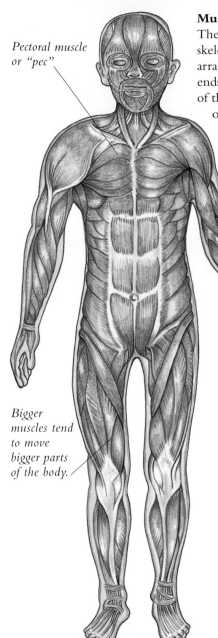

Pectoral muscle or "pec"

Bigger muscles tend to move bigger parts of the body.

Muscles galore

The body has hundreds of skeletal muscles. They are arranged in layers and their ends are joined to the bones of the skeleton. This is the outer muscle layer, just under the skin. Beneath is the middle muscle layer, and then an inner layer. Every muscle has a scientific name, but few of them have common, everyday names.

The smallest muscles are grouped in the hand.

Opposed muscles

Muscles are arranged in opposing pairs or groups. One pulls the bone one way, and the opposing partner pulls it back again. This is because muscles can contract to pull, but they cannot forcefully lengthen, to push them. A muscle's end tapers into a thin, rope-like tendon. This is joined firmly to a bone of the skeleton.

A muscle at the front of the leg contracts to bend ankle and toes.

A muscle at the back contracts to straighten the ankle and stand on tiptoe.

MOVING

Tʜᴇ muscles, bones and joints all work together to make the body move. The muscles are controlled by the brain. It sends out thousands of nerve signals every second, along the nerves to every muscle, telling them when to contract or pull, and then when to relax and stop pulling. Even simple actions like sitting or standing involve dozens of muscles. These contract or relax at exactly the correct time, by the correct amount, to keep the body's posture upright, well positioned and well balanced. As you grow up, you learn to control your muscles for everyday movements such as standing, walking, talking, running, biting and chewing. Sometimes when you are not concentrating, these actions go slightly wrong. You might bite your tongue! When you learn a new action, you have to concentrate hard, to coordinate the new movement pattern. Practice makes perfect – well, usually!

Look in a mirror and exercise your face muscles. You use them to smile, frown and make other expressions. Try contracting or stretching each one in turn, in a new and unusual way, to make some very funny faces!

Funny fingers
Try moving your fingers apart and then together in two pairs while keeping them straight, as shown. Is it easy? If not, can you soon learn to do it smoothly? What about the other hand? As this is an odd and seldom-used hand position, it is not very easy to do unless you practise.

Rub and pat
Can you pat your head while rubbing your body? How about patting your body while rubbing your head? And what happens when you swap hands, with the left one on your head, instead of the right one? Any new movement pattern seems difficult and awkward at first. But the brain soon learns to control the muscles and make the action.

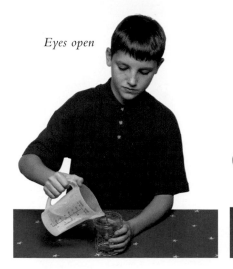

Eyes open

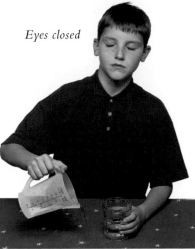

Eyes closed

The inner sense of position

You "feel" the positions of your body parts, especially muscles and joints, with your body's inner sense. You also watch your movements with your eyes, to guide them more accurately. Try pouring water from a measuring cup in one hand to a beaker in the other, with your eyes open. Easy! Now try with eyes closed. "Feel" your way using your inner sense. Splash … oh dear! Try again. Do you improve with practice?

Standing and falling

Balance is a continuous body process. The brain uses information from the eyes, skin, muscles, joints and inner ears. It sends out instructions to the muscles to keep the body well balanced. Stand still on two feet, close your eyes, lift one foot and put your arms by your sides. With less sense input, balance becomes more difficult.

Funny looks

Most of us use the same muscles every day, but if you try to make a new expression, you will be using muscles you don't normally use. So your face will feel strange as well as looking odd!

BIRTH AND BABIES

People are like their parents because they inherit genes from them. Genes are found in body cells, in the form of the chemical called DNA. Half of them come from the mother, the other half from the father. They contain instructions for growth, development and maintenance of the body. Each person has a unique set of genes, except for identical twins. The twins' genes are the same, so they look the same.

THE human body has parts and systems for many life processes, such as breathing, digestion, circulation and excretion. It also has parts for reproduction. This means making more of your own kind. Reproduction is not a vital process for the life of one body. But it is vital for humankind to continue. A woman has egg cells for reproduction in her ovaries, the special glands in the lower abdomen. A man has sperm cells for reproduction in the testes, which hang in a skin bag below the penis. When a woman and a man have sex, an egg cell and a sperm may join, or fertilize, and then begin to develop into a baby. This happens inside the female's body, in a part called the uterus or womb. After nine months of development, the baby is born, when it emerges from the womb along the birth canal into the outside world. Over the years the body grows and develops through the main stages of life, from baby, to toddler, to child, to adolescent, to mature adult.

Sperms
Sperm cells look like microscopic tadpoles. Millions are made in the testes every day.

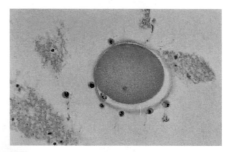

Eggs
Egg cells are huge compared to normal body cells. One ripens each month, as part of the reproductive or menstrual cycle.

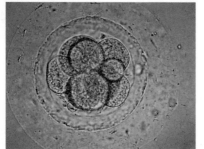

Fertilization
When an egg and sperm join, this is called fertilization. The fertilized egg becomes two cells, then four cells, then eight cells, and so on.

Developing baby

One week after fertilization, there is a microscopic ball of cells. They continue to multiply – into hundreds, then thousands, and millions. This happens inside the mother's womb. Gradually the ball of cells grows and changes shape. Two months after fertilization it is a tiny baby, the size of a thumb. It already has a heart, muscles, nerves and many other parts.

Umbilical cord

Muscular wall of uterus

Placenta

Cervix (opening or neck of uterus)

Birth canal

Inside the uterus

In the womb, it is warm, dark and wet. The developing baby is in a pool of watery amniotic fluid. It cannot eat or breathe for itself. It receives all of its food and oxygen from the mother. The oxygen and nutrients pass from the mother's blood to the baby's blood, via a dish-shaped part called the placenta (afterbirth) in the wall of the uterus. The baby's blood flows between the placenta and its body along the umbilical cord. Nine months after fertilization, the baby is well developed and ready to be born. The strong muscles in the uterus wall contract and push the baby along the birth canal. As the baby emerges into the world, it may cry, which helps it to start breathing for itself.

First feeds

After birth, the baby breathes in its own oxygen. The mother feeds her baby on her breast milk, or special milk from bottles. This milk contains all the nutrients that the baby needs in its first months outside the womb. The hours and days after birth are very important, as the mother and the baby get to know each other.

Growth

The baby grows into a child. The body is following the instructions in its genes. But the child is also learning from others, and developing into an individual with a personality, with likes, dislikes, wishes and wants. He or she begins to crawl, stand, walk, talk, run, read, write, draw, make friends, go to school, learn lessons … life is always busy!

INDEX